HOW TO BE YOUR
WIFE'S
❧ Best Friend ❧
365
WAYS TO EXPRESS YOUR LOVE

DAN BOLIN & JOHN TRENT, Ph.D.

P.O. Box 35007, Colorado Springs, Colorado 80935

Library of Congress Catalog Card Number: 95-69198
ISBN 08910-98755

Printed in the United States of America

4 5 6 7 8 9 10 11 12 13 14 15 / 99 98 97 96 95

To our best friends, Cay and Cindy

INTRODUCTION

◈

I love fly fishing. I can stand in a mountain stream from sunup to sundown in search of a twenty-inch rainbow trout. But twenty minutes into clothes shopping with Cay my legs go limp, I frantically search for a chair; finding none I turn in desperation to locate the appliance department. My strength returns, and I stand for the next hour watching a ball game as all seventy-three televisions change camera angles at the same time.

You see I'm different from Cay. For better or for worse we are very different. Our sexuality, heritage, experience, and personality have all played a part in our individual developments, which have created the wonderful uniqueness between us.

Our marriage is no masterpiece. Like most couples we struggle with our differences. The struggling takes place in two arenas: *understanding* and *acceptance*. No man or woman can fully comprehend the needs and expectations of his or her counterpart. It is important to work at understanding, but the greater challenge is to accept, appreciate, and benefit from the differences in a way that honors and celebrates the strengths and uniqueness of the other.

We bring very different values, traditions, and expectations from our family heritages. We have three options for dealing with these differences. We can (1) peacefully coexist, (2) go to war, or (3) unite to form a new and personal heritage. This new relationship builds on the strengths of each partner's experience and adjusts to redefine our unique and powerful oneness.

This new union can be illustrated by a recollection from twenty-five years ago as a high school student. The snow began to fall shortly after the school day had started. By lunchtime several inches had covered the lawns and Roosevelt High School was alive with energy. The order had come from the top "No snowballs will be thrown!"

I'm not sure how many students challenged the rule, but I can still picture the principal and vice principal standing back to back by the flagpole in front of the school. They were cold, the sky was gray and foreboding, and they anticipated attacks from every side.

Much of the time marriage is like that snowy day in Portland. Life is tough; the signs on the horizon are foreboding, and dangers appear at every side. But an ally stands with you guarding your back. A friend is there to protect your areas of vulnerability. Standing with you in the face of life's cruel attacks is one who provides strength and security.

But marriage is also like the thaw of springtime. Having stood together through winter's blasts you share new life and laughter. You dream together of adventures, share new hopes, and enjoy the strength and refreshment you draw from each other.

Many men go through life without knowing the strength of a faithful ally or the security of an accepting friend. Fewer still have a strong and secure relationship with their wives, which can be enjoyed during the times of laughter and is needed in the times of tears.

Cay and I have laughed a lot—and we have cried more than most. We were laughing our way to a family picnic when we stopped by the doctor's office for our four-year-old daughter's annual checkup. At that routine visit Catie was diagnosed with leukemia. Our laughter turned to terror, and five years later our terror turned to tears.

The statistics regarding marriages that unravel following the death of a child are staggering. The hurt, frustration, and guilt can be the toxins that poison a marriage. But every marriage has its traumas, and every person has moments when he or she defines himself or herself by the choices he or she makes.

The antidote for the deadly poisons that can destroy the marriage relationship is love. This love is not the fair weather kind that enjoys the good times but dissolves at the first hint of trouble. It is the kind of love that holds on tight when the storms of life blow. This kind of love demonstrates itself in three strong cords: *communication, courtesy*, and *commitment*.

Communication is more than transferring facts from me to Cay and back again, it is the thread that sews our hearts together. Dreams, fears, opinions, and feelings are clarified and captured as they are expressed. Listening to Cay and accepting her wisdom has built a strong bond of friendship between us. The secure walls of love allow her to vent her deepest emotions.

The more we disclose areas of vulnerability to our spouse the more that trust is allowed to grow. The story is told of a man whose wife wanted him to tell her that he loved her. The more she begged, the more difficult it became for him to say the words, "I love you." Finally he said, "I told you I loved you when we got married. If I change my mind I'll make sure you're the first to know." Communication is always difficult, but often it is more difficult for men than women.

Courtesy is the second chord of friendship. The times we have struggled the most are when I become too busy to spend special time with her, take on too many responsibilities to be sensitive to her needs, or become too rigid to say, "I'm sorry. It's my fault. Will you forgive me?" We have lived through a lot and have found that the little acts of kindness and courtesy are much more significant than big demonstrations of affection or grandiose material gifts. It is easy for me to drift into a state of insensitivity toward Cay. I come home from work with my "game face" on. I still have a "hurry up," "get it done right," "don't bother me with the details" attitude. I like to think that I have the right to "my time" when I get home. In reality I need to come home from a busy day ready to be a participant in the family rather than a spectator.

Simple acts of courtesy bind us together. Asking myself a few basic questions can adjust my mental attitude: What can I do for Cay to honor her? How can I lighten her load? What could I do that would put a smile on her face?

Courtesy requires more than an emotional feeling of love; it requires commitment.

The last chord is commitment. Some mornings I wake up and I don't want to go to work; some Sundays I don't want to go to church; some days I don't feel like doing the things it takes to be a good husband. If I did only what I wanted to do, someone else would have to change the batteries in the remote control and I might never get off the couch.

The difference between what I want to do and what I actually do has everything to do with commitment and follow through. We need to evaluate our commitments. Whether we think about it or not, we are trading our lives—every moment of every day—to fulfill our commitments. Look long and hard at any commitment that consistently takes you away from your wife or your children.

Someone has said that marriage is like being a fly on a windshield: If you are on the outside you want in, and if you are on the inside you want out. How I feel about being married has nothing to do with the promises I made to Cay over eighteen years ago. It takes no courage or tenacity to quit when things don't go our way or when our feelings are hurt or when the grass looks greener. . . . As a matter of fact the grass is not greener. As author and family advocate Tim Kimmel said, "Twenty-five percent of all men kiss their wives good-bye when they leave their house. Ninety-nine percent of all men kiss their house good-bye when they leave their wife."

The ideas in this book are designed to provide a resource for making your wife feel special and loved. They are a starting point for demonstrating your love for her. We men often have trouble understanding how important it is to demonstrate our love in a manner that will be meaningful to her. Being her best friend may be the best thing you ever do for yourself.

—DAN BOLIN

1

Send flowers for no obvious reason.

2

Check with used bookstores or collectable shops
until you find a magazine
that has her birth date on it
(like a *Life* magazine dated June 1960).

3
Put your dirty clothes in the hamper.

4
Arrange your day so that she can sleep in
while you take the kids to school
or out to breakfast.

5
Go to the zoo together.

6

Praise her publicly for her strengths,
character, and abilities.

7

Surprise her by cleaning the refrigerator
from top to bottom, inside and out
(including sweeping under and behind it!).

8

Plan a date night and keep it.

9

Drag out her high school (or college) yearbook
and ask her to tell you about
some of the people who were important
to her then.

10
Buy a new pillowcase,
and with permanent or fabric ink pens,
write an "I love you" message to surprise her.

11
Tell her she looks like she
has lost weight.

12
Say "please."

13
Share the responsibility for making sure
that the kids wear safety equipment when biking,
canoeing, etc., . . . and that you both do too!

14
Give her a present that is not "useful."

15
Bring home a specialty cooking utensil you don't presently have, one either of you can use (like a crêpe maker or a special cheese grater).

❖

16
Ask her to be your valentine.

❖

17
Say, "I'm sorry, it's my fault."

18

Throw her towel in the dryer
when she steps into the shower and then hand it
to her piping hot.

19

During the holidays
while she's out of the house,
go wild with mistletoe (fake or real),
hanging strands over every doorway, etc.
Catch her when she stands underneath it.

20

Order an unexpected late night pizza
(after the kids have gone to bed).

❖

21

Consult with friends or a visitors' bureau,
and choose four inexpensive "one day" trips you
could take near your home. (Visit a neighboring
city's aquarium; take your bikes to a mountain
preserve a few hours away, etc.) Then ask her
to pick which of the four she'd like to do together.

22

Check with her before you invite
anyone home for dinner.

23

If she loves chocolate
(only about ten wives don't),
have a surprise "chocolate party"
with a three-course meal of everything chocolate
she loves. (Include low-cal brownies
and cocoa as well.)

24
Let her control the temperature in the car.

❖

25
Ask her, "Honey, from your perspective,
what is the most important issue
our child is facing right now?"
And then ask how you can help.

26
Buy bubble bath for her.

27
When she suffers a loss or personal defeat,
put your arms around her
and even be willing to share her tears.

28
Make sure she sees the doctor
for regular checkups.

29
Wear your wedding ring.

30
Know her favorite flavor of ice cream.

31
Give her an award certificate for being
"wife of the year."

32
Write out a two-page "story of our courtship"
that recounts how you felt about her
and the circumstances of your falling in love.

33

Count to ten while you kiss her
when you come home from work.

34

Every day tell her something
you appreciate about her.

35

Go for a walk together.

36

Buy her a "sleep mask" and include
three coupons she can redeem for
"an uninterrupted Sunday afternoon nap."
(Meaning you turn the phone off and take
the kids out.)

37

Wink at her across a crowded room.

38

Take three hours one Saturday morning to clean
the shower or tub enclosure so that it sparkles
like new. (Extra credit if it's ceramic tile!)

39

Buy six valentines on Valentine's Day.
Give her one that day,
and then mail one to her every two months
throughout the year.

40

Say to her, "Honey, where's the vacuum?"
and then vacuum with a happy attitude.

41

Have a "destination unknown" evening each fall,
when you plan a whole evening
(including child care!) as a surprise for her.

42
Hold her when she cries.

43
Ask her to hold you when you cry.

44
Wake her up for a "You're beautiful
without makeup" breakfast
at a casual restaurant that's not your
usual hangout.

45
Hold her hand in public.

46
Without being asked,
tackle the closet or area
in the garage that most needs
tidying up.

47
Talk about problems.

⬦

48
Help take care of your children
when they are sick.

⬦

49
Open the car door for her.

50
Put a single red rose on her pillow.

❖

51
Get her a special polishing cloth
and cleaning spray for her glasses
or sunglasses.

52

Be excited about going to her high school class
reunion with her. Do the little things that will
make this weekend very special for her.

❖

53

Get a book that lists outstanding
"bed and breakfast" locations in your area
and call ahead for reservations.
Spend a night (or more!) together.

54
Put the toilet seat and lid down.

55
Tell her you'd marry her all over again.

56
Take time to share upcoming events with her . . .
instead of letting her find out about
your schedule when you're talking with others.

57

Call her during the day just to say "Hi."

58

Kiss her goodbye when you leave the house
in the morning . . . even if it's a gentle kiss
and she's still asleep.

59

Buy a house plan magazine
and dream together.

60

Make a habit of
"Sunday night sweetheart car checks."
That's when you check all
the fluid levels in her car
and fill it with gas.

61

Ask her to pick the video
when you rent one together.

62

Stay at the table until she's finished eating
instead of hurrying off
and leaving her to sit alone.

❖

63

Go on a picnic together.

❖

64

Praise her parents.

65

Set up a secret way to say "I love you"
in public—like taking her hand
and squeezing it three times.

66

Ask her, "What three things could we do
that would improve our relationship?"
Then talk with her in detail
about her response.

67

Read a book together.

❖

68

Not saying something critical to her when the
opportunity arises is the most loving thing to do.

❖

69

Make and mail a card to her
even when it's not her birthday.

70

Discuss with her the question
"As you look at our child(ren),
what dreams do you have for them
regarding careers and their personal lives?"

71

Let your children know they are to speak to their
mother in an honoring way. Back up your words
by watching your own tone of voice.

72
Surprise her by taking her car
to the car wash.

73
When you travel on business,
make sure she knows ahead of time
your travel route and hotel address
and phone number.

74
Pick the kids up after school.

75
Rent a boat for the day.

76
Find out from a respected hairstylist
what new product for hair has come out
and get it for your wife.

77
Remember your anniversary.

78
Never compare her cooking
to something you've eaten at 35,000 feet.

79
Keeping yourself in shape and well-groomed is a
present to both her and you.

80
Say "Thank you."

81
Keep a flashlight in your sock drawer so you can get dressed without turning on the light when you need to leave home before she wakes up.

82
Go to bed at the same time.

83
Take the lead in the "clean up" and "take down" parade on January 2nd.

❖
84
Let her pick the colors
to decorate your home.

❖
85
Use the washer, dryer, and iron yourself.

86

If you like to go to sporting events,
buy her a stadium chair with padding
and a backrest and carry it for her.

87

Don't underestimate her need to hear you say,
"I'd marry you all over again."

88
Fill the salt and pepper shakers.

89
Buy her a subscription
to her favorite magazine.

90
Be responsible for the meals for an entire
week—plan, shop, cook, and clean up.

91

Run the entire family
(even if it's just the two of you)
through a "fire drill" so that everyone will be
comfortable with a plan of action
if an emergency arises.

92

Every once in a while
fix her fresh-squeezed orange juice.

93

Buy new drip pans for the stove
when the old ones are beyond cleaning.

94

If she listens to talk radio, ask her,
"What did you hear on the radio today
that was interesting?"

95
Give her a foot massage.

96
Give her a long-distance gift certificate
so that she can call a best friend
or family member.

97
Pick a flower for her.

98
Say "no" to one committee
or outside project.

99
Make sure she has a dressy dress
that is less than two years old
. . . and then take her out once a year
to a place she can use it.

100
Rent a tandem bike and ride together.

101
Hand her the TV remote control
and let her use it as she chooses.

102
Clean the garage.

103

At some time other than Valentines
or Christmas, take out an ad
in the classified section
that tells your whole city
how proud you are of your wife.

104

Send away for a T-shirt from her high school
or college alma mater.

105

"Weather proof" and "weather strip" the house
each fall and early summer
to make sure your home is as comfortable
(heat and cool efficient)
as it can be.

◈

106

Go shopping for clothes with her
and don't give the impression that you are tired.

107
Never make a joke at her expense.

108
Wrap her birthday and Christmas presents.

109
Get her a coffee or cocoa mug,
with your and the kids' pictures on it.

110

Go together to look at
and/or purchase antiques.

111

Set aside an "I'm committed to a positive tone
of voice" jar, and put a dollar in the jar each time
you raise your voice at her.

112
Change the overhead light bulbs
when they go out.

❖

113
Ask her, "What one thing
causes you the most stress during your day?"
and then do what you can to give her a break
from that responsibility. Ask her how it's going.

114
Say, "When you do . . . I feel. . . ."

115
Pretend you've won $10,000,000
and dream with her
about what you would do with the money.

116
Browse through a bookstore together.

117
Be willing to spend the money
to get her a really good winter coat,
instead of one that she can get by with.

118
Make sure she always has change for a toll road,
parking, or a phone call.

119
Brush her hair.

❖

120
Choose a week in the not-too-distant future
and propose not to watch any television.
Take the time that would normally be spent
watching the tube and spend it with her
doing what she wants.

121
Have a picture taken of the two of you
at special occasions.

122
Take her with you on a business trip.

123
Buy six new toothbrushes,
and every three months, replace her old one
with one you purchased.

124
Keep her picture in your wallet.

125
Help each of your children write a special note
to Mom telling her just how much they
appreciate everything she does.

126
Wash the dishes.

127

Read a book out loud to each other while driving.

128

When she is sick adjust your schedule
to meet her responsibilies in the home
and care of your children.

129

Call her if you will not be home for dinner.

130

When there's a morning where there's only
enough time for one of you to exercise,
take care of family responsibilities
so that she can be the one
who gets to walk or run.

131

If she has expressed that there is an area
in her life in which she wants to improve,
go out of your way to help her grow.

132

Rent a convertible when the two of you
are taking a weekend away.

❖

133

If she almost always gets stuck
doing a certain chore,
don't forget to thank her
for all the work involved in doing it.

134
Give her a framed picture of the two of you.

135
With the hundreds of computer programs
available, get her a game, tool,
or personal organizing program she can use.

136
Sit beside her on the couch.

137
Make her birthday, Christmas,
and your anniversary special.

138
Give her a laminated card
she can use once a week for
"Thirty minutes to talk about whatever you'd
like." During this time, don't talk about anything
that is unique to you—focus on her.

139

If she's a coffee or tea drinker,
start an "I love you" club where you bring her
a small sample of a different type each month.

140

Talk through the holidays with her months ahead
of time, asking, "What would you really like
to have happen this Thanksgiving or Christmas?"

141
Use good manners.

142
Make a list of all her great qualities
and share it with her.

143
Encourage her to continue
her education.

144

If she has a favorite sports personality or team,
cut out clippings from the sports page you read
and create a scrapbook for her.

145

Take a camping trip . . . in your backyard.
Complete with barbecuing steaks, s'mores,
and a night spent out under the stars.

146
Share your dreams with her.

147
Have adequate life insurance.

148
Meet her with a rose
when she gets off an airplane.

149
Ride bikes together.

150
Encourage her to take a weekend away
with her girlfriends. (Adjust your schedule
to care for the kids while she's away.)

151
Learn the names of her friends and associates.

152
Change the filters in the heating and cooling
systems of your home.

153
Talk about and consider her opinion
in all significant financial decisions.

154
Work in the yard together.

155

Give her a "seven day affirmation list,"
on which you've named one character trait
you appreciate about her each day for a week.

156

Give her a cellular phone if she must drive
distances in the car alone.

157
Share your fears with her.

158
Leave a handmade "I love you" bookmark
in a book you know she's reading.

159
Hold her hand at weddings.

160

Find out the meaning behind her name
and have a local calligrapher write it out.
Frame it for her.

161

Be serious about making your home secure
by installing strong window and dead-bolt locks.

162

Take her to an amusement park.

163

No matter what the message is in your fortune cookie, read instead, "You have a wonderful and beautiful wife."

164

Take the initiative to register for a marriage enrichment weekend where you both can go and make your marriage the very best it can be.

165
Clean the storage room
or attic together.

166
Buy her a new nightgown.

167
Buy enough underwear and socks
that the wash doesn't have to be done too often.

168
Write her a love letter.

169
Sign you and your spouse up for a hot air balloon
ride . . . and be sure to bring your camera.

170
Cook her a candlelight dinner
and clean up afterwards.

171
Share your dessert with her
(even if it's chocolate).

172
Go in ahead of time to a favorite restaurant
and arrange for a gift or flowers to be
presented to her.

173
Discuss current events.

174
Help her update your family's
address directory.

175
Together write a year-end letter
to your friends.

176
Learn her favorites—color, food, author, artist,
restaurants, desserts, musician. . . .

177

While she's out one afternoon,
get out the face paints for you and the kids
and have her come home to a
"We're not clowning around . . . We love Mom!"
evening (complete with circus acts by the kids).

178

Take a continuing education course
together at a community college.

179

Call her on the phone and ask her out on a date.

180

Find a sport you can enjoy together—tennis, golf, swimming, fishing, skiing, hiking, jogging.

181

Get your carpet cleaned before she suggests it.

182
Keep a charged fire extinguisher
in the kitchen.

❖

183
Give her permission to tell you
if your clothes don't match.

184
Invite her family members
or friends over for dinner.

185
Walk at a pace that will allow you
to walk side by side.

186
Begin conversations with "I feel"
rather than "I think."

187
Go to almost any store and make up a "basket
of love" with several small items she will use
and enjoy—candy, coffee, candles, etc.

188
Together visit friends in the hospital.

189
Put her number first on the speed-dial
on your office phone system.

190
Take her back to the place you went
on your first date.

191
Kidnap her for a walk
through a nature trail or local park.

⬥

192
Go to a local music store and ask to see
their list of "songs in print"
(especially country songs).
Then pick ten titles
that reflect your love in words.

193

Put an "I love you" coupon
in her favorite cereal box
that will fall out when she pours
her breakfast.

194

Ask her, "How does it make you feel
when I . . . ?"

195

Lie on her side of the bed on a cold night
to warm it up for her before she gets in.

196

Select a charity you both support
and make a special year-end gift
in honor or memory of a person
you both love(d).

197
Sing together in the car.

198
Visit an art gallery with her
without complaining.

199
Pack a picnic and take her
to a concert in a park.

200
Ask her to help you remember
people's names.

201
Multiply her compliments.
When someone says something nice about her,
top it with an even nicer compliment about her.

202

Take her to a specialty restaurant
that neither of you has ever tried.
(Like a Tai or Indian restaurant, etc.)

203

Tell her not to wait up
when you call to tell her you will be home
after your regular bedtime.

204

On a cold winter night, heat up the hot water bottle or electric blanket ahead of time before she comes to bed so her side is toasty warm.

205

Go to the park and throw a Frisbee together.

206

Live within your means.

207

Find out what her God-given gifts are
and encourage her to get involved in using them.

———————— ❖ ————————

208

If you have worked without a day off for too long
take two days off in a row—the first for you
and the second for her.

209
Avoid saying "You never" or "You always"
during a disagreement.

210
Volunteer together with a local relief agency
to cook and serve meals to the homeless
during the holidays (or anytime!).

211
Turn off the television.

❖

212
Before it becomes a forced decision,
talk ahead of time with her about who will accept
the responsibility for her aging parents
. . . and yours. Plan this carefully—
you won't regret it.

213
Ask her more questions
and follow-up questions.

214
Actively support a decision she makes
with the children—in front of the children.

215
Make both sides of the bed.

216
Give her a coupon for "One chore completed
by me that you'd really rather not do."

❖

217
Compliment something
about her father or mother.

❖

218
Go to a museum with her.

219

Give her a five-minute back rub—
no strings attached.

220

Spend "quality" time with each child
as a way of loving them and encouraging her.

221

Fix breakfast in bed for her.

222

Ask her, "What one thing is lacking
in the living (dining/kitchen/family) room
that would make it seem more complete to
you?" Then work toward getting that one thing.

223

When you travel, send postcards to her
from the airport—even if they'll arrive
after you do.

224

Offer to take back something to a store
that she needs to return.

225

Well ahead of her birthday or a special occasion,
write or call several of her old (or current)
friends. Ask them all to write a letter
of encouragement for her
and send them to you at work.
Then present her the letters in a scrapbook.

226

Go to bed at the same time five nights in a row.

227

Plant a garden together . . . including
her favorite flowers and/or vegetables.

228

Give her a birthday card
that you make yourself.

229

Send for an issue of her hometown newspaper
and surprise her with it.

230

Mat and frame a picture she really enjoys.

231

Compliment something she did for you
. . . in front of the children.

232

Set up a "First Monday" lunch date where you start off the month by sharing a midday meal together.

233

When she expresses that she needs to talk to you while you're watching television, get up and push "record" on the videotape player (or wait until next week's episode!).

234

If you've raised your voice at her, after things have cooled down, take her hand and tell her, "You are very valuable to me, and I shouldn't speak to you that way."

235

Have a hot cup of coffee or tea ready for her when she comes out of the shower.

236
Paint her toenails.

237
Make it your responsibility to be sure the kids are buckled in the car before you take them anywhere.

238
Open the doors in public places for her.

239
Take golf lessons with her.

240
When your family plants a garden,
make sure you help her weed it consistently.

241
Purchase an "emergency road service" kit
for her car, making sure she knows
how to use each item in it.

242

Get a "book on tape" you know she would like
you to hear, then listen to it together
for fifteen minutes each night
until the book is finished.

243

Get a key chain for her with a picture of you
(or you and the kids).

244

Scout out which of her shoes need some
extra care and either take them in
or polish them yourself.

245

Have lunch with her on a weekday.

246

Take out the garbage *before* she asks.

247

Ask her, "What do I do that really bugs you?"
For the next thirty days make an effort
not to do that.

❖

248

Remember how important your household
pets are to her, and treat them with kindness.
(That means her cat, too!)

249
Don't argue in the bedroom.

◈

250
Leave a message on her voice mail telling her
you love her and what you appreciate about her.

◈

251
Buy her a tape or CD of instrumental music.

252

Take a vacation day from work and make it
an "I'll paint any room in the house for you" day.

253

Call every night you are on the road.

254

Give her three hugs for every one kiss.

255

Make a custom label for her favorite
refrigerated beverage that you tape to the can
or bottle, surprising her with a love message.

256

Get her a specialty item from her favorite
makeup line—something she would like,
but normally passes up.
(Ask the makeup salesperson
for suggestions!)

257

Put the cap back on the tube of toothpaste.

258

Plant a tree with her
(on your property or in a local park or preserve
that encourages planting) for the two of you
and each child in your family. Then go there
together to check on it once a year.

259
Make a jigsaw puzzle together.

260
Serenade her outside the window, complete with
a musical instrument, if you can play.
(Make sure the kids are cued in so no one calls
911 thinking there's a prowler outside!)

261

If she likes to cook, get her a one-day lesson
at a gourmet cooking school.

262

After meals, clean up the kitchen together.

263

Bake cookies for her.

264

Keep an active journal where you record
special family events, thoughtful actions she did,
or loving thoughts. (John's great uncle did this
every day for almost sixty years!)

265

When you make a promise to follow through
on a chore, errand, or commitment . . . *do it*.

266

Arrange for her to go to a massage therapist
(or legitimate masseuse) for a time of pampering.

267

Embark on a remodeling project together . . .
being sure you stay with the job long enough
to finish it as well as clean up.

268
Take country and western dance
lessons together.

269
Give her a "day to sleep in" coupon
she can cash in with one day's notice
for a morning where you get the kids up
and off to school.

270

Feed the dog without being asked.

271

When she mentions that she's due for a hair
appointment, find out which salon she likes best
and arrange for a surprise appointment
and manicure. (Pick a time
when you're covering the bases at home.)

272

Sweep and mop the kitchen floor.

273

When she is in conversation after a social event
give her a wave and smile when you're ready
to leave . . . not "that look."

274

Go to a concert together.

275

Keep your eyes open for those roadside stands
that can hold a small treasure to bring home
(like fresh fruit or wild flowers).

276

Ask her, "Do our children seem as happy
as you'd like them to be?"

277

Compliment her cooking.

278
Don't underestimate the bonding power
of loving eye contact.

279
Purchase a new pair of hiking boots for her
and then take her for a hike in the woods.

280
Tell her if her slip is showing.

281

Take time to prepare a will and estate plan
with her that you both understand
and feel comfortable with.
Keep it up to date.

282

Commit to a "Saturday morning Dad's the
chef" time when you become the chief cook
(and dishwasher!).

283

Encourage her friendships
with other women.

284

Make a "first fifteen" commitment
for two weeks. Spend the first fifteen minutes
talking to her when you wake up
and give her the first fifteen minutes
when you get home at night.

285
Stir the cookie dough
and maybe you'll get to lick the bowl.

---◈---

286
Without her help, enlist the kids
(if you don't have any, you're on your own!)
on an "everything put away by eight" campaign
where everyone squares away the major family
rooms by eight o'clock at night.

287

Like the ball team, take a break at half-time
and spend it talking with the family.
(You can always watch the highlights later.)

288

Take a wallet size photo of your wife
(and/or family) and have it laminated.
Then you're ready to pass it around
when she's not there (and when she is!).

289
Take the kids out
so she can have a leisurely bath.

290
To keep a business trip from being a parenthesis
in your relationship, share with her the key
meeting or tasks you'll be facing—
and even the times of your meetings—
as a way of making her feel connected.

291
Clean your own fish.

292
If she has a close relationship
with a brother or sister who lives out of state,
call him or her and begin planning toward
a special "surprise" visit of that loved one.

293

Go to PTA meetings together.

※

294

Make an effort to remember what she tells you
about her friends, and provide her consistent
time to be with them.

※

295

Set a regular time each week just to talk.

296

Plan ahead to attend a local parade.
Pinpoint a great spot, and then you go early to
reserve special seats.
She and the family can come later
in the morning without having to wait for hours.

297

On the days when you get out of bed before she
does, write her a note telling her you love her.

298
Take her to her favorite restaurant.

299
Call her by a pet name that acknowledges
something special you appreciate about her.

300
Help her hang wallpaper.

301
On her birthday, get a baby picture from her scrapbook (or parents) and play for her the song, "You must have been a beautiful baby."

⬧

302
Give her the choice of the aisle or window seat when you're traveling together.

⬧

303
Watch ice skating on television with her.

304

When she takes time to do her nails,
be sure to comment.
If you see that she's short on time,
get her a gift certificate
to have a manicure and pedicure.

305

Commit to reading (or listening on tape to)
two books each year
on building strong relationships.

306

Have her circle the coupons she wants to keep
in the paper and then you volunteer
to cut them out.

307

When she goes walking or jogging for exercise,
make sure you know her route ahead of time.

308

Make sure her car is in safe working order.

309

Don't eat onions for dinner. (Be sure to chew some mints before you get home if you've had garlic or even salsa for lunch!)

310

When she travels, be at the airport before her plane is due to greet her.

311

Take a weekend away, just the two of you,
without interruptions.

312

Be willing to pay the necessary expense
(or go to the extra trouble) of transporting
a favorite pet if you have to move.

313

Help her clean out a closet.

314
Make "making up" a priority
so that you end each day positively.

315
Save the cards she gives you for birthdays and
anniversaries, instead of just throwing them out.

316
Get out the suitcases for her
when she has to go on a trip.

317

When the next year's calendars
come out in the fall, get her a new one
with her birthday and your anniversary
circled in red.

318

Encourage her to write the editor
or send in a piece to the local paper
when she has a strong opinion on something.

319
Unload and load the dishwasher.

320
Arrange your schedule to go with her
to the doctor's office if she is apprehensive
about an appointment.

321
Plan a vacation together.

322

If you like to camp, or just enjoy being outside,
take a star-watching class
at a local junior college together.

323

With so many major Broadway plays on tour
across the country (like "Les Miserables"),
plan an extra special trip to see one.

324
Be on time for dinner.

325
Commit yourself to wipe around the basin
after shaving so it is as clean or cleaner
than when you started.

326
Buy quality tires for her car.

327

Challenge yourselves with a 2,000 piece
jigsaw puzzle that takes the two of you
to do . . . and keeps you close together for days
(or maybe weeks!).

328

Find out which radio station she listens to
during the day, and call in an "I love you"
request for her. (Be sure to tape your request
in case she misses it!)

329

If she has a favorite charity or cause,
offer to help her do a car wash or other fund-raiser
for that project.

330

Show respect for her father and mother.

331

Pray for her.

332

If you're certain of the way she drives to work
or errands, check with a friendly neighbor
and post a banner or hand-painted
"I love you" sign she'll see.

333

Fill her entire closet from top to bottom
with balloons with hearts drawn on them
in magic marker.

334
Go to a "potion and lotion" store and buy
a basket of "sample" shampoos, conditioners,
creams, and lotions.

335
Stop to ask for directions when you're lost
and she's in the car.

336
Watch a sunset together.

337
If it snows where you live, let her awaken one morning to a new snowfall and a huge love letter carved out in white for her to see.

338
Write a poem just for her.

339
Tell her she is beautiful.

340
Present her favorite dessert to her
as the first course in an "I love you" dinner
(when the kids are out).

341
Go on a weekend getaway
with one or two other couples.

342
If she has a hobby, collection, or interest, send
for a specialty mail-order catalog featuring items
that match her interest.

343
Bite your tongue when you start to make
a sarcastic comment.

344

Be sure to thank her parents
when you're with them
for raising such a wonderful daughter.

———————— ◈ ————————

345

Ask her, "What would you like to change
about me?" Then work on her suggestions.

346
Call her from an airplane phone
just to tell her you miss her.

❖

347
If you find a bird or small animal that has been
hurt, work together in bringing it back to health
or getting it to a shelter or vet who can help.

348
Make sure an up-to-date city map
is in the glove compartment of her car.

349
If she has a favorite historical figure,
look for a book that captures that person's life
and give it to your spouse.

350

Give her a coupon good for ten uses
on a chore she usually does.

351

Do all things without complaining.

352

Fix dinner for the family.

353

Talk a local frozen yogurt shop into making
a heart-shaped (or other unique shape) pie
for her . . . complete with cookie crust.

❖

354

Ask her, "What would constitute a perfect
evening for you?" Followup by working
to set up such a night.

355
Take ballroom dance lessons together.

356
Contact her best female friend
and arrange for a surprise getaway
where the two of them can spend a weekend
at a motel with a warm pool and lots of talking.

357
Take her to play miniature golf.

358
Arrange for the two of you
to do a service project together,
such as visiting a nursing home
or preparing "comfort kits" for the Red Cross.

359
Hang up your clothes.

360
Ask her, "Which radio station
would you like to have on in the morning?"
and set the clock radio
so that she will wake up
to that music or conversation.

361

Ask her, "What are three things I do that express love to you?" Concentrate on doing those things.

362

Ask her, "What three things would you want to happen in our relationship this year that would make it the best year of our marriage?"

363

Take her on a date on a regular basis.

364

When you say you'll be home at a certain time,
make that a priority appointment
and be on time.

365

Tell her "I love you" as often as she can stand it.